Contents

A Note About This Story

Ira Levin was born in New York City on August 27th, 1929. While he was a student at Drake University, then at New York University, he wrote plays for television. After university, Levin spent two years in the U.S. Army, where he wrote scripts for army training films.

After he left the army, Levin began to write theater plays and also short stories. Many of his stories were published in well-known magazines.

A *Kiss Before Dying* was Ira Levin's first novel. It was published in 1954 and it made him famous. The book won the Edgar Allen Poe Award. Since then, Levin has continued to write crime and horror stories.

Two films have been made of *A Kiss Before Dying* (in 1956 and 1997), and several of Levin's other stories have been made into famous films too. These include *Rosemary's Baby*, *The Stepford Wives*, *The Boys from Brazil* and *Sliver*.

Some of the characters in this story are university students. Most students at American universities study for four years. Stoddard University, in this story, is a very big *college*. There are many different buildings on its large area of land, or *campus*. Some of the buildings contain *lecture rooms*, where the students are taught by *lecturers*. Some buildings are *laboratories*, where the science students do *experiments*. Some of the students live on the campus. These students have rooms in *dormitories*. The most important teachers in the university are called *professors*.

CENTRAL LIBRARY

INVERCLYDE LIBRARIES

CENTRAL LIBRARY

This book is to be returned on or before
the last date above. It may be borrowed
for a further period if not in demand.
Enquiries and renewals tel.: (01475) 712323

INTERMEDIATE LEVEL

Series Editor: John Milne

The Macmillan Guided Readers provide a choice of enjoyable reading material for learners of English. The series is published at five levels—Starter, Beginner, Elementary, Intermediate and Upper. At **Intermediate Level**, the control of content and language has the following main features:

Information Control

Information which is vital to the understanding of the story is presented in an easily assimilated manner and is repeated when necessary. Difficult allusion and metaphor are avoided and cultural backgrounds are made explicit.

Structure Control

Most of the structures used in the Readers will be familiar to students who have completed an elementary course of English. Other grammatical features may occur, but their use is made clear through context and reinforcement. This ensures that the reading is enjoyable and provides a continual learning situation for the students. Sentences are limited in most cases to a maximum of three clauses, and within sentences there is a balanced use of adverbial and adjectival phrases. Great care is taken with pronoun reference.

Vocabulary Control

There is a basic vocabulary of approximately 1600 words. Help is given to the students in the form of illustrations, which are closely related to the text.

Glossary

Some difficult words and phrases in this book are important for understanding the story. Some of these words are explained in the story, some are shown in the pictures, and others are marked with a number like this: ... [3]. Words with a number are explained in the Glossary on pages 90 to 95.

PART ONE: DOROTHY

1

The Room Near the Campus

April 1950

Night was coming to the town of Blue River, in the state of Iowa.

It was nearly dark in the small room near the Stoddard University campus. The two people in the room that Sunday evening were both second-year students at the college. They were looking at each other in silence.

The handsome young man was angry. His plans had been working so well. And now this news had come! But he wasn't going to show his anger—that wouldn't help him. He walked to the window, and for a few seconds, he looked out at the lights of the town. He looked at the yellow lights in the streets. He looked at the red light on top of the Municipal Building[1], the tower which was the tallest building in Blue River, a mile or two away. Then he turned, and he smiled at the young woman sitting on the bed.

"Are you *sure* that you're pregnant?" he asked her gently. "Are you really sure that you're going to have a baby?"

"Yes, I'm sure," she replied. "The doctor told me that I'm two months pregnant." She started to cry. "What will we do? Can we get married soon?"

"Don't cry," the young man said. "Everything will be OK." He smiled again.

The young woman stopped crying and she tried to smile

too. "Oh, let's get married right away," she said. "I'm sure that my father will like you when he meets you. We'll be so happy!"

"Well, we *could* get married immediately," the young man said. "But this isn't what I'd planned, Dorothy—you know that. I'd planned to meet your father in New York in the summer, at the end of the college year. I wanted to ask him for permission to marry[2] you *then*.

"I want your father to like me, Dorothy," he went on quickly. "If we're already married when I meet him, he'll guess the reason. He'll guess about your pregnancy. He won't like that, he'll be angry. He'll stop giving you money. We'll be poor. I'll have to leave college and get a job in a store! And you'll have to leave college to take care of the baby. We'll have to live in a trailer[3]. How will you feel about that? How will your family feel about it?"

"I love you," the young woman replied miserably[4]. "I don't care about being poor. I don't care about my family. We'll be happy—I'm sure about that! And I don't believe that my father *will* be angry. Anyway, we don't have any choice. I'm pregnant! We'll have to get married soon."

The handsome young man walked over to Dorothy and put his arms around her. Tonight, he had to pretend to love her.

"We do have a choice," he said.

"What do you mean?" the young woman whispered nervously.

"I know someone who can help us," he replied. "You don't *have* to be pregnant, Dorothy."

The young woman pushed him away from her.

"You want me to have an abortion[5]?" she said angrily. "No! I won't do it!" And she started to cry again.

"I love you," the young woman replied miserably. "I don't care about being poor. I don't care about my family."

"Listen to me," the young man said. "I do love you, Dorothy. You know that. But I don't want to destroy your life. Your family is rich. You don't *know* about being poor. But *I* know about it. You would hate it! Listen! I want to marry you next summer, with your father's permission. Then he'll go on giving you money. We'll rent[6] a little house near the campus. It will be wonderful. But you mustn't have this baby!"

"I won't have an abortion!" Dorothy shouted.

"You won't need an operation," the young man replied quietly. "You'll only have to take some pills[7]. I can get them from a guy in one of my classes. His uncle owns a drugstore[8], here in Blue River."

He held the unhappy young woman in his arms again. For the next hour, he whispered in her ear. He told her many things that she wanted to hear. At last, he looked at his watch.

"You must go back to your dormitory," he said. "It's nearly ten o'clock. I'll meet you tomorrow evening, under the tree outside the Pharmacy Laboratory[9]. I'll meet you at eight o'clock. I'll bring the pills then."

———

When his girlfriend had gone, the handsome young man put his hands over his face.

"Oh, God!" he said desperately.

He'd planned everything so carefully! But he'd been careless about *one* thing. He'd only made love with[10] Dorothy once. He'd had to make her believe that he loved her. But he'd been careless. And now she was pregnant!

"I *can't* marry her if she's pregnant!" he told himself. "I will *not* live in a trailer with Dorothy and a baby."

The young man was desperate because he *wanted* to marry

Dorothy Kingship. He wanted to marry her because she was rich. He wanted to marry her because her father was the owner of Kingship Copper Incorporated. When the young man had found out that a young woman in his Economics and Philosophy[11] classes was one of Leo Kingship's daughters, his life had changed. He had begun to think of an exciting future for himself. He had thought of a future with lots of money, a beautiful house, and a good job with Kingship's big, successful company.

Soon after meeting Dorothy, he had written to the offices of Kingship Copper and asked for some information about the company. The Kingship offices in New York City had sent him some brochures[12]. He kept them at the bottom of a drawer in his desk. Every night, he took the brochures out and he read them. Every night, he looked at the photos of the great Kingship smelting works[13] in Illinois, and he read about how much money the company had earned in the last year.

The handsome young man wanted a good future very much. His early life had not been easy. He had been born in the little town of Menasset, near Fall River, Massachusetts. He was an only child—he had no brothers or sisters. His parents had been poor. His mother had hated her husband because he had never had a good job. Her son had become the most important thing in her life—she was interested only in him. His father was dead now, and his mother still thought that the young man was the most important thing in her life.

By the time he was eighteen, the young man had started to believe that all women were like his mother. Lots of women had been interested in him. They liked him because he was very handsome. Usually they were older women, with plenty of money. They had enjoyed making love with him. But their interest in him had never lasted very long. Each time, another handsome young man had replaced him after a few months. Now, he hated women, but he was still happy to spend their money.

"Why did Dorothy get pregnant?" he asked himself angrily. "She's a stupid young fool!"

The young man was twenty-four years old—five years older than Dorothy. He was older than most of the other students at Stoddard University. He had been in the U.S. Army for a few years before he came to Stoddard. He had fought in the Far East in 1945, the last year of the war. That was where he had learned that it was easy to destroy lives.

Although he was angry with Dorothy Kingship, the young man suddenly felt a little sorry for her. She was a very possessive[14] person. And possessive people were difficult people to like! The week before, Dorothy had told him about another of her boyfriends—a Stoddard student who she'd spent a lot of time with. This student had broken up with[15] her before Christmas because she'd become too serious and too possessive about *him*. "Possessive women frighten men!" the young man thought.

But he understood the reason for Dorothy's possessiveness. Her early life had been very different from his. Dorothy was not an only child—she had two sisters. But her parents had been unhappy, like his. After the first years of her marriage, Dorothy's mother had been in love with another man for a short time. Eight years later, Leo Kingship found out about this relationship. He had not been able to forgive his wife. He divorced[16] her, although by then she was very ill. The three girls stayed with their father, and soon after the divorce,

10

their mother died. Leo Kingship had never been a kind, loving father. And after her mother's death, Dorothy was afraid of being alone. She had always tried to make people like her. She still did that.

Dorothy had told the handsome young man, "I'm sure that my father will like you when he meets you." But she had often talked about her father. He was a hard man. He never forgave people if he thought that they had done wrong. The young man was sure that Leo Kingship would never forgive his youngest daughter for getting pregnant. And he would never forgive her if she got married without his permission.

"What will I do if she won't have an abortion?" the young man asked himself.

There was one thing that he was happy about. He had always met Dorothy secretly. Neither of them had told any of the other students that they were meeting each other in the evenings. He didn't think that any of them knew about the relationship. And he was sure that Dorothy hadn't told her family about him yet.

Although Dorothy had two older sisters, she didn't see them very often. The eldest sister, Marion, had a job in New York City, where Leo Kingship also lived. Dorothy never wrote to Marion or phoned her. Ellen, the middle sister, was at Caldwell College. Caldwell was a hundred miles from Blue River, in the state of Wisconsin. The young man knew about the sisters, because Dorothy had told him a lot about her family. And he knew that at Christmas, Dorothy had argued with Ellen. They hadn't spoken to each other since then.

"Dorothy won't tell anybody else about the baby," the young man told himself. "If the pills work[17], everything will be OK."

2

The Pharmacy Laboratory

On Monday evening, the young man met Dorothy on the campus, near the Pharmacy Laboratory. He gave her the two white pills that he had gotten from his friend.

"You must take both of them," he told her. "Take them tonight. You'll probably have a fever for an hour or two. And you'll probably throw up[18]. But then, you'll abort the baby."

"What will we do if the pills don't work?" Dorothy asked him nervously.

"Don't worry, darling," the young man replied. He smiled. "If they don't work, we'll get married right away."

Dorothy put the pills in her pocket.

"Do you want to go to a movie tonight?" she asked.

"I'm sorry, I have to do a lot of work for my Spanish class," the young man said.

"I'll help you," Dorothy said quickly. "I'll come to your room with you." Dorothy was good at Spanish—she was a student in an advanced Spanish class.

"No. I'll be OK," he said. "Go home and take the pills now. Then you'll be OK in the morning."

Dorothy didn't understand. The handsome young man wasn't good at Spanish, but usually he didn't care about it. Why did he want to do extra work for his class now? And why wouldn't he let her help him? She was puzzled.

Dorothy didn't argue with him. She went back to her dormitory. She sat on her bed, and she looked at the two big white pills.

"I could lie to him," she said to herself. "He would never find out about it. I could tell him that I'd taken the pills and that they didn't work. If I did that, he'll marry me soon. We'd be happy, whatever my father says."

But Dorothy didn't want to lie to her boyfriend. They were going to get married soon. And lying wasn't a good way to start a marriage. She got a glass of water from the bathroom, closed her eyes and took the pills.

An hour later, she had a fever and a terrible pain in her stomach. After another hour, she threw up. But the next morning, she was still pregnant.

———

On Tuesday morning, at two minutes after nine, the handsome young man was sitting in a lecture room on the campus. He wasn't really listening to what the Philosophy lecturer was saying. He was thinking about Dorothy. Where was she? She was a Philosophy student too, but she hadn't come to the lecture this morning. Was that good? The friend who had sold him the pills hadn't been sure that they would work.

"If your girlfriend is two months pregnant, it might be too late," he'd said. "These pills are really for people who are only a few weeks pregnant. But she can try them, can't she?"

"Perhaps she aborted the baby in the night," the handsome young man thought nervously. "Perhaps Dorothy isn't feeling well enough to come to classes this morning."

But at a quarter after nine, the door of the room opened quietly and Dorothy came in. She was very pale. She sat down next to the young man and put her books on her desk. She wrote a few words on a page of her notebook, tore out the page, and passed it to him.

The pills didn't work. I had a fever and I threw up all night, but I'm still pregnant.

The young man closed his eyes. He tried not to show his anger and despair. After a moment, he opened his eyes again and he smiled at Dorothy. He quickly wrote a few words on a page of his own notebook.

Don't worry. We'll get married this week.

He smiled at Dorothy again and he showed her the page. But he didn't tear it out of the notebook.

The young man was thinking hard. Dorothy would want to get married right away. He needed some time to think of another plan.

"Oh, God," he thought. "I wish that the pills had killed her!" And as soon as he had thought that, something inside him changed. Suddenly, he felt calm. He was in control of his future again.

When the class ended, the two young people left the lecture room together.

"We have to talk," the young man said. "Let's go into the town center. We can have some coffee there. I won't go to any more classes today. And you don't have any more classes till the afternoon."

Dorothy was still pale, but she was happy and excited.

"Let's get married tomorrow," she said.

"No, that's too soon, darling," the young man replied. "We have to find somewhere cheap to live. We can't live in my little room. There's a trailer park on the other side of town. Some of the married students live there. I'll talk to somebody about renting one of the trailers. We'll get married on Friday. Then we can have a weekend together at a hotel and move into the trailer on Monday."

"Do we *have* to wait till Friday to get married?" Dorothy asked.

"It's only a few more days," the young man said.

"OK. I'll write to my sister Ellen tonight," Dorothy said. "I'd like to tell her my news right away."

"That's not a good idea, Dorothy," the young man said. "If you tell Ellen about our plans, she'll tell your father about them. He might try to stop our wedding. You can phone your family after the wedding on Friday."

They argued for a couple of minutes. But finally, Dorothy agreed. The two young people walked to the town center. They drank coffee in a little restaurant there. Then Dorothy left the restaurant to go back to the campus.

The young man watched her leave.

"I'm going to have to kill her," he told himself. "But everybody must think that her death is an accident. Or perhaps a suicide—yes, people must think that she killed herself. Poor Dorothy!"

———

Half an hour later, the young man was sitting in the university library. On his desk were books about famous murders, and books about toxicology[19]. He read them quietly for a while, writing notes in his notebook. When he left the library, he had a list of five poisons. Any one of them would kill a person quickly. Now he had to get a small amount of one of these poisons. Drugstores were not allowed to sell poisons, but the young man knew one place where he could get them—Stoddard University's Pharmacy Laboratory.

The young man had never been into the laboratory, but he knew that there was a storeroom for chemicals in its basement. All the chemicals which were needed for the

Pharmacy students' experiments were kept there. And the final-year students had keys to the storeroom. The final-year students often did experiments without a teacher. The young man had to get into that room. So he'd have to pretend to be a final-year Pharmacy student.

From the library, he walked to the campus bookstore. On the wall of the store was a list of the books which students studied for their classes. He looked at the list for a minute. Then he bought a copy of the textbook which all final-year Pharmacy students had to use. It was a tall thin book with a green cover. He bought some white envelopes too.

A quarter of an hour later, the young man was standing in the basement corridor of the Pharmacy Laboratory. He was pretending to read the notices on a bulletin board[20], which was next to the locked door of the storeroom. He was holding the tall green textbook under his arm, together with a note-book and the envelopes.

He wanted one of the real Pharmacy students to open the storeroom door for him. But that wouldn't be a problem. There were hundreds of Pharmacy students. Soon, one of them would come to the storeroom. The student wouldn't recognize the young man, but this wouldn't be a problem either. They couldn't all know one another. There were three large final-year Pharmacy classes. Whoever came to the storeroom would see the young man standing in the corridor with the final-year textbook. Whoever came would think that he was a final-year student—but a student in a different class. The young man told himself this and he tried to look calm and relaxed. But he was very nervous. He didn't plan a murder every day!

After a few minutes, a pretty female student came along

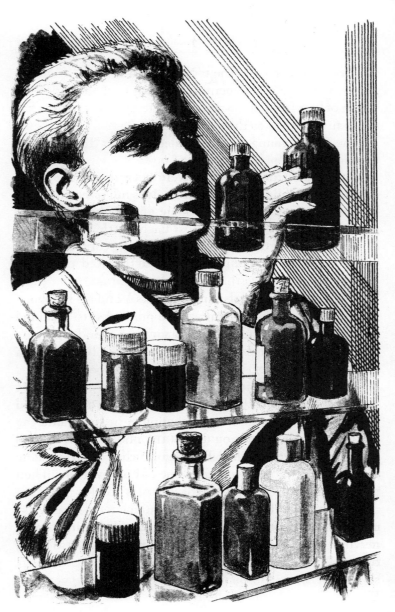

In a minute, he had found the bottle that he was looking for.

the basement corridor. She took a bunch of keys[21] from her purse. At the same moment, the young man took his own bunch of keys from his pocket and pretended that he was trying to find the key to the storeroom.

The pretty young woman smiled at him. "I'll open the door," she said.

And a moment later, they were both inside the storeroom. All around the room were shelves full of bottles. The bottles contained chemicals. Some of the chemicals were powders, and some were liquids. Each bottle had a white label with black letters, which identified the contents. Some of the labels also had the picture ☠ and the word 'POISON' in red letters.

The young man put the green textbook and his notebook on a desk. He opened them and he pretended to read and take notes. Soon, the young woman had found what she wanted. She put some powder from one of the bottles into a small glass container. Then she went to the door.

"Goodbye," she said, as she left the room.

As soon as she had gone, the young man started to read the labels on all the bottles. In a minute, he had found the bottle that he was looking for. WHITE ARSENIC (As_4O_6) ☠ POISON was written on the label. He opened the bottle and he poured some of the powder into one of his envelopes. Then he found a bottle of empty gelatin capsules[22] and he put a few of them into another envelope. A minute later, he was walking away from the Pharmacy Laboratory. He was no longer nervous. He was calm and relaxed again. His plan was going to work!

3

The Note

That evening, in his small room near the campus, the young man made the arsenic pills. Each empty gelatin capsule had two pieces—a smaller one and a larger one. The young man carefully opened two of the capsules. He carefully filled the two smaller pieces of gelatin with arsenic powder. Then he carefully pushed the larger pieces of gelatin over the smaller ones.

He had read about white arsenic in the toxicology books. He knew that the amount of arsenic in the two capsules was about ten times the lethal dose. They contained ten times the amount of arsenic which was necessary to kill someone.

Now he had the pills! But he hadn't started to think about the next part of his plan. He had to make Dorothy take the pills. Well, that wouldn't be too difficult. But unless the police believed that Dorothy had killed herself, they would start asking questions on the campus. They would ask where the poison had come from. Then perhaps the pretty young Pharmacy student might remember seeing a stranger in the storeroom. The police would show her photos of all the students in Dorothy's classes. That mustn't happen! He had to make Dorothy write a suicide note[23]. That was the difficult problem.

When he went to bed that night, the young man still didn't have a solution[24] to his problem. And he didn't have much time to find one. He had told Dorothy that he'd marry her on Friday. If he didn't marry her by Friday afternoon, she would become suspicious[25]. She would write to her sister Ellen and tell her about the baby. Then he'd have to leave

college and move to another state. And that wasn't the
future that he'd planned for himself. But he wasn't going to
live in a trailer with a wife that he didn't love, and a noisy,
smelly baby! Dorothy would have to die before Friday afternoon!

———

The next day was Wednesday. All morning, the handsome
young man worried about his problem. He found the solution
during the last class of the afternoon.

The last class was Spanish. The students were studying a
romantic novel called *La Casa de las Flores Negras*. The young
man hated the book. But while he was trying to translate a
passage from the novel, he found the solution to his problem.
And as soon as he found it, he was very happy.

When the Spanish class ended, he met Dorothy by the
Pharmacy Laboratory and he took her to a movie. After that,
they went to a restaurant. They had coffee and cheeseburgers.

"Dorothy," the young man said, as she finished her coffee.
"Will you lend me the photo that I gave you? I want to get a
copy of it for my mother."

Dorothy opened her purse and took out a small photo-
graph of the handsome young man. The words "To Dorothy,
with all my love" were written across the bottom of it. She
gave it to him.

"I'll give it back to you next week," he said.

"OK. But please take care of it," she replied. "I want to
keep it forever!"

When they left the restaurant, the young man took her
back to his room and made love with her. He felt sorry for
her. This was only the second time that they had made love,
but it would be the last time too.

As soon as she had gone back to her dormitory, the young man burned the photo. He didn't want the police to find anything that connected him with Dorothy.

The young man's first class on Thursday was Economics. Dorothy was a student in this class too. She came into the room as the lecturer was starting to speak. She sat next to the young man, and she smiled at him happily.

The young man wrote some words on a page of his notebook. He showed them to Dorothy.

> *Please take notes for me. I have to finish some*
> *Spanish translation for my class this afternoon.*

Then for twenty minutes, he pretended to write a translation of a passage from *La Casa de las Flores Negras* in his notebook. At the end of that time, he stopped writing and he looked very puzzled for a minute. Then the young man tore a small piece of paper from his notebook. He quickly drew a picture of Dorothy on one side of it. Then he turned it over. On the other side, he wrote some words.

> *Can you help me? I don't understand this.*

> *Querido,*
> *Espero que me perdonares por la infelicidad*
> *que causaré. No hay ninguna otra cosa que puedo*
> *hacer.*

He passed the piece of paper to Dorothy. She read the words quickly. Then she turned the paper over. She was going to write the translation on the back. But she saw the drawing, and she smiled.

She turned to a new page in her own notebook and wrote the translation on that. She tore the page from the book and passed it to the young man. And as he read it, he knew that everything was going to be OK.

> *Darling,*
>
> > *I hope that you will forgive me for the unhappiness that I will bring to you. There is nothing else that I can do.*

Now he had Dorothy's suicide note!

During the afternoon, the young man went to a room on the campus where there were several typewriters[26]. Any Stoddard student could use these. He typed an address on one of his white envelopes.

> *Miss Ellen Kingship*
> *North Dormitory*
> *Caldwell College*
> *Caldwell, Wisconsin*

She tore the page from the book and passed it to the young man.

The young man met Dorothy after her last class of the afternoon.

"I've just talked to my friend—the friend whose uncle owns the drugstore," he began. "He told me that he gave me the wrong pills on Monday." The young man took an envelope from his pocket. "These are the right ones," he said. "You must take them tonight."

"But I don't *want* to take any more pills," Dorothy said nervously. "I want to get married tomorrow."

"Dorothy, listen to me!" the young man said. "If we have this baby now, it will grow up in a trailer. It will have a bad start in life because its parents will be poor. Please, take the pills, Dorothy. We'll get married soon anyway. But I want to meet your father first. Then we'll have some money. We won't have to live in a trailer. We can live in a real house. We'll be so happy. And we can have a baby next year, darling."

"No," Dorothy said miserably. She started to cry. "No, no!"

"Dorothy, please do this for me," the young man said, putting his arms around her. "I know that you want the baby. But you're only thinking about yourself. You aren't thinking about me or the child. Don't give our first child a bad start in life." Suddenly, his voice was cold. "If you won't take the pills Dorothy, I won't marry you. You'll have to ask your father for help. What will *he* say?"

They talked for half an hour. Finally, Dorothy took the envelope from him.

"Take the pills at about ten o'clock this evening," the young man said. "If these pills don't work, I'll marry you tomorrow afternoon. I promise you that!"

Then he held her hand for a moment and he left her. Slowly and sadly, she walked towards her dormitory.

———

At a quarter after ten that night, the handsome young man went to a telephone booth[27] in the street near his room. He phoned Dorothy's room at the dormitory.

"Did you take the pills?" he asked her.

"Yes," she said. "I took them at ten o'clock."

"Thank you, darling," he said. "My friend said that you will probably feel some pain half an hour after you've taken them. You mustn't worry about it. Don't tell anybody. The pain will soon go. You'll be OK in the morning. Goodnight, darling. I'll see you tomorrow."

"Goodnight," she replied. "I love you."

The young man put Dorothy's translation from *La Casa de las Flores Negras* into the envelope with her sister Ellen's address on the front. Then he dropped the envelope into a mailbox[28]. He smiled as he walked back to his room.

4

The Municipal Building

The handsome young man was early for his first class on Friday morning. The Philosophy lecturer hadn't arrived yet. Three girls were talking in a corner of the room. They were excited about something, and the young man was worried. Were they talking about Dorothy? Had somebody found her dead body already? That would be bad! Dorothy's sister Ellen wouldn't get the note until after three o'clock that afternoon. If Dorothy's body was found before that, the police would come to the campus and ask all the students in Dorothy's classes questions.

The young man had hoped that nobody would start to worry about Dorothy until the evening. As soon as Ellen got the note, she would phone the University Office[29]. Then the police would be sure that Dorothy had killed herself, even before they went to the dormitory. Then they wouldn't ask questions in her classes.

The lecturer arrived and everybody sat down. The handsome young man tried to forget his worries. He tried to listen to the lecturer's words. After a few minutes, he heard the door of the room open and he heard somebody come in. He didn't turn his head. But when somebody sat down next to him, he looked around. Suddenly he wanted to scream. His skin felt cold and he thought that he was going to throw up.

Dorothy smiled at him and passed him a piece of paper. He waited a few moments, then he read the words on it.

The new pills didn't work either.

"Oh, God," the young man thought desperately. "Why did I trust her? She didn't take the pills! She wants to get married right away, so she didn't take the pills! And at three o'clock, her sister will get the note. Then she'll phone the campus. And then there'll be trouble!"

He stopped listening to the lecturer and he started to think hard about his problem. The suicide note was on its way to Caldwell—he couldn't change that. He looked at his watch. It was ten o'clock. The note would reach Dorothy's sister's dormitory at three o'clock that afternoon.

"So in the next five hours, Dorothy has to die," the young man told himself. "And everybody must think that she killed herself. What can I do?"

But soon, he had an idea and he felt calm again. Dorothy believed that she was going to be married that afternoon. And people in Blue River often got married at the Municipal Building. The Marriage License Bureau[30] was there. People had to go to the bureau to get a license before they could be married. And there was a judge's office in the building too. If two people didn't want to marry in a church, the judge could marry them, as soon as they had their license.

"And the Municipal Building is the highest building in the town," the young man thought. "It's fourteen stories high. If someone jumped from the top of it, they would certainly die!"

———

At the end of the Philosophy class, the young man spoke quickly to Dorothy.

"We'll get married today, darling," he said. "Will you wait for me by the Pharmacy Laboratory? I have to call somebody. I won't be long. Then we can make our plans."

The young man went to a phone booth. He asked the operator for the number of the Marriage License Bureau. He dialed the number.

"Is this the Marriage License Bureau?" he asked, when somebody answered. "When is the bureau open today, please?"

The clerk told him that the bureau would be open until twelve o'clock, and then from one o'clock to five o'clock in the afternoon. The bureau would be closed for an hour between twelve and one. That was when the clerks went out for their lunch.

A few minutes later, the young man met Dorothy outside the laboratory. She looked nervous. He smiled at her.

"We'll get married right away, darling," he said. "Don't worry about the baby. Everything will be OK."

"Oh, I'm so happy that you aren't angry about the baby," she replied. "I want to marry you so much."

"We have to go to the Municipal Building to get the license," the young man said. "Let's go there at about half past twelve. You'll have to show a clerk your birth certificate[31]. Don't forget to bring it."

"OK. I have to get some clothes from the dormitory and I have to buy some gloves," Dorothy replied. "I'll meet you here at a quarter after twelve."

She kissed him and she walked quickly away.

———

When Dorothy met him again, she was wearing a beautiful green suit, a green belt, a white blouse, a blue scarf and white gloves. She had put on some bright red lipstick.

"My birth certificate is in my purse," Dorothy said. "I'm so happy!"

They rode on a bus towards the town center.

It was twenty to one when they arrived at the Municipal Building. As they reached it, the young man saw something that worried him. He'd never looked at the building carefully before. Now he saw that the sides of the fourteen-story tower were not completely straight. Stories seven to twelve weren't as wide as stories one to six. And the top two stories weren't as wide as stories seven to twelve.

"If the roof of the twelfth story is very wide, I might have a problem," the young man told himself. "Everything is going wrong today!"

The two young people entered the building. In the lobby[32], they looked at a list of the offices on each story. The Marriage License Bureau was on the sixth story. They got into an elevator and they went up.

They got out of the elevator at the sixth story, and they quickly found the door of the Marriage License Bureau. There was a sign on the door. The bureau was closed until one o'clock.

"I'm sorry, Dorothy," the young man said. "I'm so stupid. Why didn't I check?" Then he smiled. "I have an idea," he said. "Let's try to get up to the roof. The view from there must be wonderful."

They walked back to the elevator and they went up to the fourteenth story. When they got out, they saw an iron door opposite the elevator. The young man pulled it open. Beyond the door were some iron stairs. The young man closed the door behind them and they started to climb. At the top of the stairs was another iron door. It hadn't been opened for a long time, and it didn't move easily. But the young man pushed it very hard, and at last it did open.

Dorothy and the young man smiled at each other as they walked out onto the roof.

"We're so high up here!" Dorothy said.

Near the door was a tall metal frame. At the top of this was the red light which the young man could see from his window every night.

The handsome young man looked around him. Each side of the roof was about 150 feet wide. All around the edge was a brick wall, about three and a half feet high and a foot thick. But the building wasn't solid. In the middle, it had a big square air shaft[33]. Each side of the air shaft was about 30 feet wide. There was a brick wall around the air shaft too. It was the same height and thickness as the outer wall.

"Come to the edge, Dorothy," the young man said. Look at the view of Blue River." He led her to the outer edge of the roof.

While Dorothy was looking out over the town, the young man looked down. Only two stories below them was a wide stone ledge. It was the roof of the twelfth story.

"If she only falls onto that roof, she won't be killed," he thought. "I'll have to push her into the air shaft."

He led Dorothy back towards the middle of the roof. He leaned over the wall of the air shaft. The sides of the shaft were straight. He could see the ground, fourteen stories below him. Suddenly he felt good. "Nothing else will go wrong," he told himself. "Everything will be OK now."

"Let's sit on this wall and smoke a cigarette while we wait," he said. "The bureau will open again in fifteen minutes."

He took Dorothy's purse and he put it down near the wall. He lifted her up, until she could sit on the wall. Then he got up too and sat beside her. He lit cigarettes for both of

them. They smoked silently for a few minutes. Then they talked about their future in the trailer park.

"It *will* be fun," Dorothy said. "We'll have a home of our own." She finished smoking her cigarette and dropped the end of it onto the roof next to the wall. The young man looked at the cigarette end. He saw the red lipstick on it. He smiled and he threw his own cigarette end into the air shaft.

He jumped down. Dorothy was still sitting on the wall. The young man held both her hands. "I'm so happy that those pills didn't work, darling," he said. "You're right! It *will* be fun in the trailer!"

"Do you really think that?" she asked. "Are you really happy that the pills didn't work?"

"Yes, Dorothy," he replied. "I want to have this baby too. I know that now." He smiled.

This was the time to push her. But there was something the young man wanted to hear first. He was going to kill her anyway, but this would give him an extra reason. He knew what she was going to say next.

"There's something I must tell you," Dorothy said. "I lied to you. I didn't take those pills last night. I threw them into the toilet. I wanted to get married to you so much. Will you forgive me, darling? I—"

Her last word turned into a scream of terror as the young man pushed her with all his strength. She fell backwards off the wall into the air shaft, screaming as she fell.

The young man was already running towards the iron door when he heard Dorothy's body hit the bottom of the shaft. Three minutes later, he was in the street. He was walking slowly away from the Municipal Building. After another minute, he saw an ambulance going towards the building.

She fell backwards off the wall into the air shaft.

PART TWO: ELLEN

1

On the Train

March 1951

I t was nine o'clock in the morning. Ellen Kingship was sitting in a train, on her way to Blue River, Iowa. She had been writing a letter to Bud Corliss. Bud was her boyfriend. Like Ellen, he was a student at Caldwell College. Ellen started to read what she had written.

> *Dear Bud,*
>
> *I'm going to be away from Caldwell for a few days. Please don't worry about me. I have decided to travel to Blue River. There's something I have to do there. Perhaps I should have told you about it before I left. I didn't tell you because I wanted to start it on my own. You asked me not to go to Blue River again. I know that you were trying to help me. I know that you didn't want me to be upset. I hope that you won't be angry with me, Bud. And I hope that you'll help me when I need your help.*
>
> *I've often told you how unhappy I was when my sister died, nearly a year ago. And you know that since I first met you at Caldwell last fall, you have made me feel much happier. You've been so good to me, Bud. But I can't stop thinking about Dorothy. I've been thinking about her death a lot recently, and I've discovered something terrible! My sister didn't kill herself—she was murdered!*
>
> *You will say, "That's stupid! The police said that Dorothy*

Ellen Kingship was sitting on a train, on her way to Blue River.

killed herself. The police know best." But the police don't know some things that I know now.

It's true that Dorothy's death couldn't have been an accident. The wall around the air shaft of the Municipal Building was more than three and a half feet high. Dorothy couldn't have fallen into the air shaft accidentally! But why did the police think that Dorothy killed herself? There were four reasons.

1) I had received a note from Dorothy on the day that she died. The police said that it was a suicide note. But there was something wrong about that letter. Dorothy had never called me "Darling". She always wrote "Dear Ellen" or "Dearest Ellen". And the letter didn't really talk about suicide. It only said that something which Dorothy was going to do was going to make me unhappy. The letter said that she was sorry for that.

2) The police found Dorothy's purse at the top of the Municipal Building and her birth certificate was in it. The police said, "She left the birth certificate there so that we could identify her easily."

3) The police also found the end of a cigarette with Dorothy's lipstick on it at the top of the building. They thought that she had gone to the top of the building, smoked a cigarette to make herself calm, then jumped into the air shaft.

4) The doctor who looked at her dead body discovered that Dorothy was two months pregnant. So the police thought that she had killed herself because she was pregnant. None of the newspaper reports of Dorothy's death said that she was pregnant. That was because our father paid people to keep that information out of the newspapers! The police knew that. They knew that he hated the idea of unmarried women being pregnant. So the police thought that Dorothy was afraid to tell our father about the baby.

Dorothy was going to have a baby, so she must have had a

boyfriend. None of her friends knew who the child's father was. They hadn't seen her with a boyfriend since Christmas. But she was two months pregnant in April, so she must have had a relationship with someone until February, at least. My father said, "It isn't strange that this man hasn't told the police about his relationship with Dorothy. He must know that she was pregnant. If he talks to the police, they will say that Dorothy's death was his fault." I agreed with this at the time. And I wasn't surprised when the police didn't try to find the father of Dorothy's child. Making somebody pregnant isn't a crime in this country!

And I wasn't surprised that Dorothy hadn't told me about her pregnancy. We'd argued at Christmas, and she hadn't written to me since then. But I did wonder who the father of her baby was. A few weeks before we argued, Dorothy told me about a student who she liked a lot. He was in her English class. She said that he was tall, blond, and very handsome. Was he the father of the baby?

The police thought that my sister had killed herself, so they weren't interested in any of her boyfriends. And there were some other things that the police weren't interested in—some very strange things. The police didn't know Dorothy, so they didn't understand that these things were strange! But in the last few weeks, I have tried to understand these things.

Ellen stopped reading for a moment.

"Bud will be angry with me for visiting Blue River," she thought. "But he'll understand. He *will* help me when I need his help."

She started reading again.

A few hours before Dorothy died, she borrowed a belt from one of her friends in the dormitory. Why did she borrow a belt, if she was going to kill herself? The police asked themselves that, but they didn't think the question was very important. They said, "She was unhappy. She didn't know what she was going to do."

But there was another question which the police didn't ask themselves. I took Dorothy's things from her room at the dormitory after her death. I found something there which puzzled me. Dorothy had owned a belt exactly like the one that she had borrowed from her friend. It was still in her room. So why did she borrow her friend's belt?

When she died, Dorothy was wearing a pair of new white gloves. She had bought them at a store in Blue River on the morning of the day she died. They were very cheap gloves and they weren't very pretty. But in her room, Dorothy had a beautiful pair of expensive white gloves. Why did she buy a cheap pair of white gloves that day, when she already had a beautiful pair in her room? The police talked to the owner of the store where Dorothy had bought the gloves. The woman said that Dorothy had first asked for a pair of white stockings. The store didn't have any white stockings, so she bought the white gloves instead. The woman said, "I think that she wanted something new that day. She didn't care whether it was a pair of stockings or a pair of gloves."

Dorothy was wearing a beautiful green suit that Friday. It was her best suit and she was very proud of it. But she was also wearing a very old white blouse. The blouse didn't look good with the suit—it was the wrong style. And Dorothy had several much newer white blouses in her room. They would have looked good with the suit. Dorothy was very careful about her clothes—she dressed very nicely. So why was she wearing that old white blouse?

And there was another strange thing. When she died, Dorothy was wearing a bright blue scarf with her green suit and her brown shoes. The scarf didn't look good with her other clothes. And Dorothy had some scarves in her room which would have looked good with the green suit.

For weeks now, I have been asking myself these questions— "Why did Dorothy borrow the belt from her friend, when she already owned one exactly like it? Why was she wearing that old blouse with her new suit? Why was she wearing the blue scarf? And why did she buy a new pair of white gloves when she already had some better ones?"

I asked myself these questions, and I told myself, "There is a message here from Dorothy. You must try to understand the message!"

Then two days ago, I asked myself the questions in a different order. I asked myself, "Why was Dorothy wearing the old blouse? Why did she buy the new gloves? Why did she borrow the belt? And why did she wear the blue scarf with her green suit?" And suddenly I did understand!

Bud, do you know the old poem about what a bride has to wear on her wedding day? The poem says that if she wears these things, she will be lucky. The poem says that a bride must wear—

> Something old, something new,
> Something borrowed, something blue.

The police said that Dorothy had gone to the Municipal Building because she wanted to kill herself. They said, "She wanted to jump from a high building, and the Municipal Building is the highest building in the town." But I've discovered something else. The Municipal Building is also the building which contains the

Marriage License Bureau. That's where people go if they want to get married. And if someone wants to get married, they have to show a clerk at the bureau their birth certificate! And now I've looked again at Dorothy's letter to me. Her words might be saying that's she's sorry for getting married without telling me first.

There's one more thing. I've discovered that the Marriage License Bureau closes between twelve and one o'clock each day. It was ten minutes to one when Dorothy fell from the roof.

I now think that this is what happened last April. Dorothy had told her boyfriend that she was pregnant. He told her that he was going to marry her. On the day she died, he told her that he was taking her to the Marriage License Bureau. Then he took her to the top of the Municipal Building, because the bureau was closed for lunch. He waited while she smoked a cigarette, then he pushed her into the air shaft!

Well, Bud, all this is the reason why I have left Caldwell for a few days. I'm on my way to Blue River. I'm on the train now. I'm going to talk to the Professor of English at Stoddard University. I'm going to be a detective! I want to find out about handsome blond students in Dorothy's English class. I want to discover who Dorothy's boyfriend was.

Don't worry about me, Bud. I'll be very careful. I've seen lots of movies where a brave girl detective discovers the identity of a murderer. She always tells him that she knows the truth about him. And he says, "Now you know the truth, so I'm going to kill you!" If I find Dorothy's boyfriend, I won't talk to him, Bud. I only want to know who he is. Then I'll tell my father about all this, and my father will talk to the police.

Ellen finished reading what she had written and she looked out of the window. The train was arriving at Blue

River. In the distance, she could see the Municipal Building. She added a few words to her letter.

I'll write to you again soon. I might know more by then. Wish me luck, Bud!

> *Love from*
> *Ellen*

2

The Two Blonds

Ellen quickly found a hotel in Blue River and she took a room for a few days. She unpacked her bag, then she phoned the English Department at Stoddard University. She spoke to the Professor of English, and told him that she was Dorothy Kingship's sister. She said that she wanted to talk to him about Dorothy. The professor remembered Dorothy, and he agreed to meet Ellen at one o'clock.

Ellen wanted to ask the professor if there had been any handsome blond students in Dorothy's English class. But she couldn't tell him, "I think that one of your students is a murderer!" The professor wouldn't believe her. She needed to give him another reason for her questions—a reason that he would believe. She thought for a few minutes, then she had an idea.

———

At one o'clock, Ellen was talking to the Professor of English. He was a kind man. He wanted to help her.

"A week before she died," Ellen began, "Dorothy told me that she had borrowed some money. She'd borrowed it from one of the students in her English class. She was angry with our father, and she didn't want to ask *him* for the money. And she only needed it for a few weeks. Recently, I looked at all of Dorothy's checkbooks[34]. I discovered that she didn't repay that money. Now my father and I want to repay it for her."

"Yes, I understand that," the professor said.

"But we have a problem," Ellen went on. "We don't know the name of the student—Dorothy didn't tell me his name.

41

And he hasn't tried to talk to us. Maybe he didn't want to ask us for the money after Dorothy killed herself. Maybe he is a kind person who didn't want to make us unhappy."

"Ah yes, you do have a problem," said the professor. "How can I help you?"

"Dorothy didn't tell me this student's *name*," Ellen replied. "But I know that he was in the same second-year English class as Dorothy. And she told me that he had blond hair, and that he was tall and very handsome. If there are only a few male students from that class who are blond and handsome, I'll try to talk to all of them."

The professor thought for a moment. "Come with me," he said.

He took Ellen to the University Office and he asked her to sit down. Then he went to a large closet and he took out about forty brown folders.

"The students from your sister's English class are in a third-year class now," he said. "These are their personal files[35]. There are photos of the students in these files."

The professor looked quickly into each folder, and he put them into two piles on the desk. "Those are the female students," he said pointing to the bigger pile. Then he pointed to the other pile. "These seventeen folders are for the male students."

Next he looked more carefully through the male students' files. He divided them into two groups. "There are seventeen men in the class," he said. "But twelve of them have dark hair. So there are only five blonds."

Then he removed three folders from the group of five.

"Nobody would call *these* three gentleman handsome," the professor said, smiling. "So now we have two handsome blond males. Here are their names and addresses."

He opened the two folders at their first pages and put them in front of Ellen. She copied the students' names and addresses into a notebook.

Gordon C. Gant
1312 West Twenty-sixth Street

Dwight Powell
1520 West Thirty-fifth Street

She gave the files back to the professor.

"Why don't you write down their phone numbers too?" he said. He read them to her and she added them to her notebook. Then she stood up.

"Thank you, Professor," she said. "You've been very kind."

———

When Ellen called Gordon Gant's number, the phone was answered by a woman.

"Is Gordon there?" Ellen asked.

"No, he isn't!" the woman replied suspiciously. "He's gone out. He'll be out until late this evening."

"Who am I speaking to?" Ellen asked politely.

"I'm Mrs Arquette," the woman replied. "This is my house. Gordon rents a room here. Can I give him a message?"

"No, thank you," Ellen said. "I'll call again later."

She put the phone down. She thought for a minute.

"If I go to Mrs Arquette's house, maybe she'll talk to me," Ellen said to herself. "I'll pretend to be one of Gordon Gant's relatives. I'll ask this woman about Gordon's girlfriends. Maybe she'll tell me who he was meeting last winter. Then I won't have to talk to him myself."

———

Half an hour later, Ellen rang the doorbell of the house at 1312 West Twenty-sixth Street.

The woman who opened the front door was small and thin. She had untidy gray hair. Ellen smiled at her.

"You must be Mrs Arquette," Ellen said. "Is Gordon here?"

"No, he isn't here," the woman said suspiciously. "Did he know that you were coming?"

"Yes. I'm Gordon's cousin," Ellen said. "I wrote him a letter. I told him that I'd be in Blue River today. I told him that I'd come to visit him for an hour."

"He didn't tell me about it," Mrs Arquette said. "Maybe he didn't get your letter. But please come in and sit down for a while. I'm happy to meet one of Gordon's relatives. Gordon's a fine young man." The woman smiled suddenly. "Come into the living room," she said. "I'll make some coffee."

Ellen followed her into the house.

"Gordon's at the radio station," Mrs Arquette said when they were sitting in her living room, with coffee in front of them. "Did you know about his radio program?"

"He did tell me something about it," Ellen replied.

"He's a disc jockey[36] on the Blue River radio station," Mrs Arquette said. "He plays records for two hours every night, except Sundays. Gordon's a very busy young man. He's at college most of the day, then in the evenings, he's on the radio!"

"No, he isn't here. Did he know that you were coming?"

"Is he happy now, Mrs Arquette?" Ellen asked. "I think that he was very *un*happy a year ago, when I last saw him."

"I don't remember that," the woman replied. She thought for a moment. "No, I don't remember that."

"I think that he'd broken up with a girl—someone he liked a lot," Ellen said. "I think that her name was Dorothy. Do you remember a girl named Dorothy?"

"No, I don't," said Mrs Arquette. "He met lots of girls, but he didn't have one special girlfriend. And I don't remember anyone named Dorothy."

Suddenly Ellen wanted to leave the house. She wasn't going to learn anything here. She stood up.

"Well, I'll go now," she said. "Thank you for the coffee."

"Aren't you going to wait for Gordon?" Mrs Arquette said. "He'll be back in a few minutes."

"In a few minutes? But you told me that he'd be out until late this evening," said Ellen. "You told me *that* when I phoned." As she spoke the words, she knew that she had said the wrong thing.

"Was that you who phoned earlier?" said Mrs Arquette. "You didn't say that you were Gordon's cousin when you phoned. Gordon gets lots of calls from girls who hear him on the radio. They all want to talk to him and meet him. I always tell them that he'll be out all day."

Now the woman was suspicious again. "But if you thought that Gordon was going to be out all day, why did you come here?" she said. "I don't believe that you're Gordon's cousin. Who are you?"

At that moment, they heard the front door open, and someone came into the house.

"I'm back, Mrs Arquette!" a man's voice called.

The woman ran out of the room. Ellen heard her whispering to someone, "She says that she's your cousin, but I don't believe her!"

Then the living room door opened, and a tall handsome young man entered. He had short blond hair. He looked at Ellen and she looked at him. Then the young man smiled.

"Cousin Hester!" he said. "I'm happy to see you."

3

The Detective

Ellen ran past Gordon Gant and Mrs Arquette, out of the front door, and into the street. She saw a taxi and she waved her arm at it. The taxi stopped and she jumped in. She told the driver the address of her hotel, then she lay back in the seat. Her body was shaking.

Half an hour later, sitting in her hotel room, she was feeling a little better. But she was angry with herself.

"I was so stupid," she thought. Her afternoon had not been successful. She hadn't discovered anything which helped her. And now, because of the lies she had told, she wouldn't be able to speak to Mrs Arquette again. And she wouldn't be able to speak to Gordon Gant again.

"I can try to find out about the other man, Dwight Powell," she told herself. "But if I find out that Powell *wasn't* Dorothy's boyfriend, I'll have to go back to Caldwell. Because if Gordon Gant *is* the murderer, he won't let me discover anything new. He'll know what I'm trying to do. And if he *is* the killer, he might try to kill *me*."

From her purse, she took the letter which she had written to Bud on the train. She put it on a table by the window. She had decided to add a few more lines to it before she mailed it.

At that moment, someone knocked on the door of her room. "Clean towels for you," said a high female voice. Ellen opened the door.

"Hello again," said Gordon Gant. "I can pretend to be someone else too!" He pushed past her into the room and closed the door behind him.

"Please don't shout for help," he said. "If you do, I'll tell the police about your visit to Mrs Arquette's house. I won't hurt you. I followed your taxi here because I want to know what's happening. Why were you pretending to be my cousin? Why did you ask Mrs Arquette those questions about me?"

"I can't tell you," Ellen said. "Please leave me alone." She was terrified.

But as she spoke, Gant saw the letter on the table by the window. He picked it up, ran into the bathroom and locked the door. Ellen started to cry.

"Please don't read that letter," she said miserably, through the door. "It's private!"

Gant didn't reply.

Five minutes later, he came out of the bathroom. He gave Ellen the letter.

"I understand now," he said. "I'm sorry. Am I on your list of handsome blond students?"

"Yes," said Ellen quietly.

"What's your name?" Gant asked her. "Please tell me."

"I'm Ellen Kingship," she replied.

"Listen to me," Gant said. "I didn't know your sister. I saw her in English class, but until she died I didn't know her name. I didn't kill her. There were other blond men in that class, Ellen. But I'd like to help you. Will you *let* me help you?" He smiled at her.

Ellen wanted to believe his words. But she had to be sure. The man who killed her sister must have been a good actor, because Dorothy had trusted him. Perhaps Gordon Gant was acting now.

"No," she replied. "I can't let you help me."

There was a book on the table next to the bed. Gant

"Please don't read that letter, it's private."

picked it up.

"You don't trust me," he said. "But I swear on this Bible[37] that I didn't kill your sister."

"No, I *don't* trust you," Ellen said. "If you *had* killed her, you'd swear on twenty Bibles that you weren't the murderer."

"That's true," Gant replied sadly. "OK, I'll go now."

After Gordon Gant had left, Ellen thought about him. Gant hadn't tried to hurt her, and she didn't really believe that he was the murderer. Dwight Powell was probably Dorothy's killer. She had to find out about him.

She sat down with her letter to Bud. She picked up a pen and wrote the address of her hotel after her signature. Then she added a few lines to the letter.

I've got a nice room in this hotel in Blue River. The Professor of English was very helpful. I think that I know now who killed Dorothy. His name is Dwight Powell and he lives at 1520 West Thirty-fifth Street. I'm going to find out about him tomorrow.

Ellen went down to the lobby of the hotel and mailed the letter. Then she went back to her room. She filled the bath with hot water and she sat in it for an hour, listening to the Blue River radio station. She heard Gordon Gant's voice on the radio. And when she heard him say, "The next record is for my good friend Ellen from Caldwell," she smiled.

The next morning, Ellen phoned the house where Dwight Powell lived. The owner of the house answered the phone.

"Dwight is working this morning," the woman said, when Ellen asked for Powell. "He has a job at Folger's Coffee Shop[38] in the town center."

Ellen made a decision. She was almost sure that Powell had been her sister's boyfriend. She would go to Folger's Coffee Shop and talk to Powell about Dorothy. If he didn't know that she was Dorothy's sister, he would have no reason to lie to her.

Ten minutes later, Ellen walked into the coffee shop. It was clean and pleasant. Powell was working behind the counter. Ellen had seen his photo in his student file. She recognized him immediately.

She sat down at the counter.

"I'd like a coffee and a cheeseburger, please," she said.

As she ate, Powell started to talk to her.

"I haven't seen you here before," he said. "Do you live in Blue River?"

"I've been here a few days," Ellen replied. "I want to get a job here. I'm a secretary."

Powell seemed a pleasant, quiet young man. But Ellen remembered that Dorothy's killer was a good actor. They talked for ten minutes about Powell's life as a student at Stoddard University. But he didn't talk about anybody named Dorothy until Ellen had finished her meal.

"When you walked in, you reminded me of someone," he told her. "And I've been trying to remember who you remind me of. Now I *have* remembered. She was a girl in my class. Her name was Dorothy. She was a nice girl." He smiled sadly.

As Ellen stood up to leave, Powell said, "Are you free this evening? Can I take you to a movie?"

She thought for a moment. Maybe she could find out more about this young man.

"OK," she said. "I'd like that."

He told her that he would come to the lobby of her hotel

at eight o'clock.

"What's your name?" he asked.

"Evelyn Kittridge," she replied.

"OK," Powell said. "I'll see you at eight o'clock then, Evelyn."

———

Ellen was sitting in the lobby of the hotel at half past seven. She didn't want Dwight Powell to ask the clerk about someone named Evelyn Kittridge!

At five to eight, Powell arrived. He took Ellen to a movie theater in the town center. During the movie, he put his arm round her shoulders. And as they left the theater, he kissed her.

After the movie, the two young people went to a restaurant for some coffee. Then Powell took Ellen back to her hotel. They sat in the lobby and talked for a while.

"You told me this morning that I reminded you of somebody," Ellen said. "Her name was Dorothy. Please tell me about her, Dwight."

"She was a very nice girl," Powell replied. "She was in my English class. She was my girlfriend for a few months."

"Why did you break up with her?" Ellen asked.

"She was very possessive," Powell said. "She got too serious about me. She wanted to get married. She was a nice girl, but I didn't want to marry her."

They talked for a few more minutes. Then Powell stood up.

"May I meet you again tomorrow night?" he asked. "We'll go to a dance."

"OK," Ellen said. "I'd like that. Come here at half past seven."

Powell kissed her, and he left the hotel.

Ellen went to her room. She was in bed when the phone rang. She picked it up. She heard Gordon Gant's voice.

"I've been worried about you," Gant said. "I thought that you might be in danger. Have you talked to any other handsome, blond English students?"

"Yes," Ellen replied. "I talked to Dwight Powell. He's a strange person. He talked about somebody named Dorothy. He said that she was his girlfriend for a short time. I'm sure that he was talking about my sister. I think that *he* killed her. He said that this girl wanted to get married, but he didn't want to marry her. Maybe that's *why* he killed her!"

"Maybe you're right," Gant said. "Are you going to meet him again?"

"Yes," Ellen replied. "I'm going to meet him again tomorrow evening. But don't worry about me. I'll be safe. He doesn't know who I am. I told him that my name was Evelyn Kittredge. Tomorrow, I'll ask him some questions about Dorothy's death. Maybe he will tell me something that he couldn't have read in the newspapers. Then I'll be sure that he was the murderer."

"Please be careful, Ellen," Gant said.

"OK. I'll be careful," Ellen said. "Thank you for playing a record for me. Goodnight."

4

On the Roof

The next afternoon, Ellen went to the Blue River Municipal Library. She stayed there for several hours. She read all the reports of Dorothy's death that had been printed in the Iowa newspapers. If Dwight Powell told her anything about Dorothy's death that *hadn't* been printed in the papers, she would know. She would know that he was the killer.

That evening, Ellen was again waiting in the lobby of the hotel when Dwight Powell arrived.

"I'm sorry, Dwight," she said to him. "I can't go to a dance this evening. I have to visit an attorney[39] in the Municipal Building. He might have a job for me. He told me that he'd be there until half past eight. Will you come with me, please? I won't have to talk to the man for long. After I've seen him, we can come back here and have a few drinks together."

"OK, Evelyn," Powell said. "I'll go." He didn't look happy.

Ellen and Powell got out of the elevator at the fourteenth story of the Municipal Building.

"The attorney's office is Room 1405," Ellen said. "It must be around the corner." She started to walk along the corridor and Powell followed her. She had phoned the office that afternoon. The attorney's secretary had told her that the office closed at five o'clock. She hoped desperately that nobody would be there now.

They soon found Room 1405. A sign on the door said FREDERICK CLAUSEN—ATTORNEY. But the office was closed, and there were no lights on inside it.

Ellen looked at her watch angrily.

"It's only eight o'clock," she said. "When I spoke to Mr Clausen on the phone this afternoon, he told me that that he would be here until half past eight! I'll have to come back tomorrow."

They walked back along the corridor. Then suddenly, Ellen pointed to an iron door, opposite to the elevator.

"That must be the way to the roof," she said. "Let's go up there, Dwight. The view will be wonderful at night. I want to look at the stars."

"Why don't we go to the dance, Evelyn?" Powell said nervously. "We still have the time to do that."

"No, I want to go to the roof!" Ellen said. She opened the door and she started to run up the iron stairs. Powell followed her slowly.

A minute later, they were on the roof. Ellen was looking up at the night sky.

"Isn't it a beautiful night?" she said to Powell. "The moon is so big! There are so many stars! Don't you love it up here, Dwight?"

"I don't like high places, Evelyn," Powell replied miserably. "I don't feel safe up here."

Ellen walked to the outside edge of the roof and looked over the wall.

"Are you afraid of falling, Dwight?" Ellen said. "I heard that one of the Stoddard students was killed here last year. I read that she fell from the top of this building. Did she only fall two stories onto that roof? Did that little fall kill her?"

"She didn't fall," Powell said quietly. "She jumped. And she didn't jump there. She jumped into the air shaft."

Ellen's skin felt cold. "He knows something about Dorothy's death," she thought. "But he could have read that in the newspapers."

"Did you know the girl who died, Dwight?" she said aloud.

"Please, Evelyn, I don't want to talk about it," Powell replied.

"But *did* you know her?" Ellen asked again.

Powell waited a moment before he spoke.

"Yes," he said sadly. "I knew her. She was the girl that I was telling you about yesterday. She'd been my girlfriend. I've always thought that Dorothy's death was my fault. I broke up with her because she was getting too serious. Then a few months later, she killed herself."

Suddenly, Ellen was very angry. She wasn't afraid of this man.

"You're lying!" she shouted. "Dorothy didn't kill herself! You *murdered* her. You made her pregnant and then you killed her! You pushed her into that air shaft!"

Powell was frightened now, Ellen could see that. But he was puzzled too.

"Pregnant?" he said. "Was Dorothy pregnant? I didn't know that. The newspapers didn't say that she was pregnant. Is that why she killed herself? Oh God, that's terrible!"

"She didn't kill herself!" Ellen screamed. "*You* killed her. You killed my sister!"

"Your sister?" Powell said. "Who are you? Why have you brought me here?"

"My name is Ellen Kingship," Ellen said. "And I brought you here because I want to know the truth. Don't try to kill me too! Somebody knows that I'm here with you. If we don't go down to the street in the next five minutes, he'll phone the police."

"I won't try to kill you, Miss Kingship," Powell said sadly. "I've never killed anybody. Please tell me something. How long had Dorothy been pregnant?"

"You *know* how long she'd been pregnant!" Ellen shouted. "She was two months pregnant when she died. That's why you killed her."

"Two months," Powell said quickly. "Oh—then the baby wasn't mine, Miss Kingship. I broke up with Dorothy before Christmas, 1949. In January, 1950, I went to college in New York City for a year. I wanted to get away from Blue River. I didn't want to see Dorothy again. I was in New York when she died. I can prove that! Someone else made Dorothy pregnant that winter."

Suddenly, all Ellen's anger disappeared. She believed him.

"I—I'm sorry, Dwight," she said.

"I'll take you back to your hotel," Powell said quietly.

———

Half an hour later, Ellen and Powell were sitting in a quiet corner of the hotel lobby.

There were screens[40] around their little table. They didn't see the man who was sitting at a table on the other side of one of the screens—the tall man in a dark coat and a hat who was listening to their conversation. They were still talking about Dorothy, but now Ellen was sure that Powell wasn't her sister's killer.

"A few days after I broke up with Dorothy, I saw her with another student," Powell said. "He was tall and handsome— he looked a little like me. Somebody told me that Dorothy had been to the movies with him a few times. We had broken up, and Dorothy wanted someone to love her. She wanted

58

They didn't see the tall man in a dark coat and a hat who was listening to their conversation.

that very much. I wasn't surprised that she found someone else so quickly."

"Who was he, Dwight?" Ellen asked. "Perhaps *he* was the father of the baby. Perhaps *he* was Dorothy's killer!"

"I don't remember his name," Powell said. "He wasn't in our English class. I didn't know him. Someone told me that he was in the same Economics class as Dorothy. And someone did tell me his name once. I wrote it in a notebook. I can't remember it now. But if we go to the house where my room is, I'll find the notebook for you."

"OK, let's go now," Ellen said. "I'm sorry that I made you go up on the roof tonight, Dwight. Dorothy's death wasn't your fault."

The two young people got up to leave the hotel. They passed the table on the other side of the screen, but it was empty. The tall man in the dark coat had already left.

Dorothy went to a phone booth. She called the Blue River radio station. She wanted to talk to Gordon Gant. But the woman who answered the phone told her that Gant was busy.

"Can I give him a message for you?" the woman asked.

"Yes," Ellen replied. "Please tell him that Ellen Kingship called. Tell him, 'Dwight Powell isn't the man.' Tell him, 'Powell knows about another student who might have been my sister's boyfriend—a student who wasn't in her English class.' Tell him that I'm going to Mr Powell's room now to find the name of this student. And please tell Mr Gant that I'll call him later."

_____

The house where Dwight Powell lived was empty when he arrived with Ellen. He made them both some coffee and he took Ellen into the living room.

"Wait here," he said. "I'll go up to my bedroom. The name that you want is in one of my old college notebooks. I won't be long."

Powell ran up the stairs and into his clean, tidy bedroom. He opened a drawer in his desk and he took out a pile of notebooks. He started to look through them.

"The name's in one of these," he said to himself.

There was a tall closet in one corner of the room. Powell didn't see its door opening slowly. He didn't see Dorothy Kingship's killer inside the closet. He didn't see the man who was aiming a gun at him.

———

Ellen heard a loud noise in the room above her. She ran out of the living room and towards the stairs. At the top of the stairs she saw a tall, handsome man. She didn't see the gun in his hand. She didn't see it because she was looking at his smiling face.

"Darling, what are you doing here?" she asked him. "What's happened to Dwight?"

"I asked you not to come to Blue River, Ellen," Bud Corliss said. "You should have listened to me!"

Then he shot her three times. The third shot ended her scream of terror.

PART THREE: MARION

1

New York City

September 1951

M arion Kingship lived alone in a small apartment in New York City. Everything in it could have told a visitor to the apartment about Marion's tastes[41]—her taste in books, her taste in pictures and her taste in music. But the only visitor who ever went to the apartment was Marion's father. He didn't go there often. And Leo Kingship wasn't interested in his daughter's tastes.

Marion had never really liked her father. She was ten years old when her parents divorced. Marion had been very upset about it. Ellen was only six then, and Dorothy five. The younger girls hadn't really understood why their mother had left them. But Marion *had* known. She'd decided then that her father was a cruel, cold man. And her mother's death, soon after the divorce, had increased Marion's dislike of him.

Marion had lived with her father and her sisters at Leo's beautiful house in New York City until she finished college. She had been a student at Columbia University, in New York. After college, she moved to the small apartment where she now lived.

Marion had always wanted to work in an advertising agency[42]. When she left college, her father had tried to make her work for the agency which looked after his company's advertising. He told the director[43] of the agency to give his daughter a job. But Marion had never wanted her father's help. She found a job with a much smaller advertising agency. She didn't earn much money there, but she liked the job and she was happy.

After she moved into her own apartment, Marion visited her father's house for dinner one evening a week. They were always polite, but they didn't really like each other. Soon after Marion left Columbia University, Ellen went to Wisconsin, to study at Caldwell College. And a year later, Dorothy went to Iowa, to study at Stoddard University. So Marion and her father were usually alone together for these weekly dinners.

Nothing had changed between them after Dorothy's death. Leo was angry because Dorothy had been pregnant. And he was angry because she had killed herself. He had paid people to keep the news of the pregnancy out of the newspapers. Then he tried to forget about his youngest daughter. After Ellen's murder, Leo did try to be kinder towards Marion. And she felt sorry for her father. Now she went to his house three evenings a week, instead of one. She tried to like him more. But she was always suspicious when Leo tried to be kind. She didn't really trust him.

Marion Kingship didn't really love anybody. But she had her apartment, and she loved that. Every Saturday, she spent the day cleaning it. And she often dreamed that one day, a good, kind man would visit her there—someone who would love her and take care of her. "Will he ever come?" she often asked herself.

———

One Saturday morning in September, Marion was cleaning her apartment. She was cleaning a table and she was looking up at her copy of Charles Demuth's painting, *My Egypt*, which hung on the wall above it. Demuth was her favorite painter, and *My Egypt* was her favorite painting.

The phone rang. Marion answered it.

"Hello," she said.

"Hello," said a man's voice, which Marion did not recognize. "Are you Marion Kingship?"

"Yes," Marion answered. "Who are you, please?"

"My name is Burton Corliss—Bud Corliss," the man replied. "I knew your sister, Ellen."

"Yes, Ellen told me about you, Mr Corliss," Marion said. Marion remembered Ellen's excitement when she had spoken about this man at Christmas. "I love him so much, Marion," her sister had said. "He's so good and kind."

"I'd like to meet you, Miss Kingship," Bud Corliss said gently. "I have a book which belonged to Ellen. She lent it to me a week before her death. I'd like to give it to you. May I bring it to your apartment?"

Marion thought quickly. This man wanted to give her something which had belonged to her sister. That was kind of him. But she didn't want him to come to her apartment. The apartment was waiting for the special man who would visit her one day.

"I'm sorry, Mr Corliss, I have to go out soon," she lied. "Perhaps I could meet you this afternoon? I'm going shopping on Fifth Avenue. I could meet you in that area at three o'clock."

"Good," replied the young man. "I'll wait for you by the statue outside Rockefeller Center. Then we'll have a drink together. Goodbye, Miss Kingship."

"Goodbye," Marion said. She put down the phone.

Marion wasn't happy about the phone call. Saturday was her special day. She didn't want to go out. She didn't really want to meet any of Ellen's friends. And she didn't want any of Ellen's books. Ellen had never liked the kinds of book that Marion liked. Marion enjoyed books by Proust, Flaubert, and all the great nineteenth-century novelists. Ellen had liked silly modern stories—stories that didn't have much meaning.

"I won't stay with this man for long," Marion thought.

———

Bud Corliss recognized Marion Kingship when she was a hundred feet away from where he was standing. She looked like both her sisters.

He took her to a bar and he bought drinks. They sat at a small table and he gave her Ellen's book.

"I read it," he said. "But I didn't like it very much. It isn't the kind of book that I enjoy. Ellen's taste in books was very different from mine. Books like this don't have much meaning, do they? I like books by Proust, Flaubert, Dickens— writers like that."

Marion smiled. "I like them too," she said.

"Ellen told me that you work for an advertising agency," Bud said.

"Yes, that's right," Marion replied. "And you're still at Caldwell?"

"No, I left college," the young man replied.

"But at Christmas, you were a third-year student, like Ellen, weren't you?" Marion said. "Why didn't you stay for your final year?"

"Well, my father died a few years ago," Bud replied. "And my mother had to get a job. She cleaned people's houses.

Bud Corliss recognized Marion Kingship. She looked like both her sisters.

Now, I don't want her to work any longer, so I've come to New York and I've got a job here. Maybe I'll go back to college next year and finish my studies then."

A few moments later, Marion stood up.

"I have to go now, Bud," she said. "Thanks for the drink."

"Won't you have another one?" Bud asked.

"I have to meet somebody else now," she lied. "It's a business meeting. I mustn't be late for it."

Bud watched Marion Kingship leave the bar. Very carefully, he followed her. He saw her go into an apartment building. He waited for half an hour, but she didn't come out again.

"A business meeting!" he said to himself. "No—she lives there."

He started to walk towards the poor part of the city where he rented a little room. He knew where Marion Kingship lived now. He could hide in the street near her building whenever he wanted to. He could follow her wherever she went.

———

For months after he had killed Ellen Kingship, Bud Corliss had been angry and afraid. He'd been angry about the time he'd spent on the Kingships—first on Dorothy, then on Ellen. And he'd been afraid about his future. Was he going to be poor, after everything he'd planned? He'd wanted some of Leo Kingship's money so much. And everything had gone wrong! He hadn't wanted Dorothy to get pregnant. And he'd *told* Ellen not to go back to Blue River, but the stupid fool wouldn't listen to him.

Bud wasn't afraid of the Blue River police. He was sure that they would never connect him with the murders. He'd been very careful. When Ellen's letter arrived, he'd decided that he had to do something quickly. Ellen had almost learned the truth about him and Dorothy! From a closet in his room, he'd taken the gun that he'd had since his years in the army. Then after dark, he'd stolen a car in Caldwell and driven it to Blue River. After he'd killed Powell and Ellen, he drove quickly back to Caldwell. He'd stopped for a moment on a bridge, to throw the gun into the Mississippi River. Yes, he'd been very careful! He'd worn gloves at Dwight Powell's house. The police wouldn't find Bud's fingerprints there! And he'd left the car near the place where he'd stolen it.

In the weeks after the killings, Bud read the Iowa newspapers every day. He read about the police investigation into the murders. He soon realized that the police weren't going to discover the identity of the killer. And he read about a man named Gordon Gant, who had lost his job as a disc jockey at the Blue River radio station. Gant had tried to tell both the police and Ellen's father that he had some information about the killings. He'd tried to tell them that Dorothy Kingship's death was a murder, not a suicide. And he'd tried to tell them that Ellen had been investigating her sister's death. The police hadn't believed him, so Gant had started to say rude things about them on his radio program. The owner of the radio station had been angry about that, and the disc jockey lost his job. Bud wasn't worried about Gant—he couldn't *prove* anything!

But when the college term finished in June, Bud went unhappily back to his mother's house in Menasset. That summer, he argued with his mother every day. He was rude and angry all the time. Then one night, he had an idea. Perhaps the time he'd spent on Dorothy and Ellen *had* been useful.

They were dead now, but *Marion* Kingship was still alive. And Leo Kingship was still a rich man!

Bud knew a lot about Marion Kingship. Dorothy had talked about her, and Ellen had talked about her. He'd spent hours listening to both of them talking about their family! Marion was very different from her sisters, he knew that. She liked serious novels and classical music. She liked the paintings of artists whose names he had never heard before.

Bud had taken a piece of paper and written on it all the things that he knew about Marion Kingship.

MARION KINGSHIP

She likes

> BOOKS: *Proust, Flaubert, Dickens etc.*
>
> PLAYS: *Bernard Shaw, Tennessee Williams*
>
> MUSIC: *Stravinsky, Bartók*
>
> PAINTERS: *Renoir, Van Gogh, Hopper.*
> *Her favorite painter is Charles Demuth*
> *(Check spelling—is it Demeuth?)*
>
> FOOD: *She likes Italian and Armenian food best.*

Things to do

> *Read books on painters.*
> *Read Proust, Shaw and Flaubert.*
> *Find out about Italian and Armenian*
> *restaurants in New York.*

After he had written the list, Bud put it in the small metal strongbox, where he kept his most private things. His brochures from Kingship Copper Incorporated were in it too. He locked the box and hid it in a closet in his bedroom.

The next day, Bud told his mother that he was not going to return to Caldwell College in September.

"I want to go to New York," he'd said. "I'll get a job there. I've had a really good idea. I can't tell you about it yet—it's a secret!"

His mother had smiled at him.

"You always have wonderful ideas, Bud," she'd said.

———

On the Sunday afternoon after her first meeting with Bud Corliss, Marion Kingship was sitting in one of the big, bright rooms in the New York Museum of Modern Art. She often came to the museum on Sundays. It was her favorite place in the city. She was looking at some large statues, when she heard a noise behind her.

"Hello again, Marion," said Bud Corliss. "I didn't expect to see you here."

Bud was lying. He *had* expected to see Marion there. He had been waiting near her apartment building when she came out, and he had followed her to the museum.

"I love this museum," Bud went on. "I often come here."

This was a lie too. Bud had been there only once before. He'd found the rooms which contained paintings by the modern artists that Marion liked most.

"I come often too," Marion said. She smiled at the young man.

"I always wanted Ellen to be interested in art," Bud said. "But she never wanted to go to museums or look at paintings. Ellen was a very sweet girl, but her tastes were so different from mine. I liked her very much, but I don't think that we would have stayed together after college." He looked sad for a moment. Then he smiled.

"Let's look at the paintings together," he said. "I love American paintings. My favorite artist is an American. His name is Charles Demuth. Do you know his work, Marion?"

―――

Several hours later, as the two young people left the museum together, Bud held Marion's hand for a moment.

"I'd like to take you to a restaurant for dinner tonight," he said. "There's a wonderful Armenian restaurant, not far from here. Do you like Armenian food, Marion?"

2

Gordon Gant

December 1951

It was December 24th—Christmas Eve. Marion Kingship looked at the newspaper she was holding and she smiled. Tomorrow, it would be Christmas Day. And a few days after that, it would be her wedding day. At last, she was going to be happy!

She read the story in the newspaper again.

MARION KINGSHIP WILL BE MARRIED ON SATURDAY

Miss Marion Kingship, the daughter of Mr Leo Kingship, will be married on Saturday. Mr Kingship is the owner of Kingship Copper Incorporated, one of the most successful companies in the U.S. Miss Kingship will marry Mr Burton Corliss.

Mr Corliss was in the U.S. Army during the Second World War, and later he studied at Caldwell College, Wisconsin. He now works in the offices of Kingship Copper. Until last week, Miss Kingship worked at an advertising agency.

Marion smiled again. The last few months hadn't been easy for her. At first, her father had been suspicious of Bud. "That young man doesn't love you, he loves my money," Leo said, after Marion told him about Bud. "First he tried to get the money from Ellen. Then she was killed. So now he's trying to get it from you! I'm going to find out more about him."

"If you do that," Marion had replied angrily, "I'll never speak to you again!"

Her father understood that she would do what she had said. He promised not to investigate Bud's life. Ellen told him that she and Bud wanted to get married. She told Leo that they loved one another. "We'll be so happy together," she'd said. "We like all the same things. We like the same books and plays and paintings. We even like the same food!"

At last, Leo changed his mind about Bud and about the marriage. "My wife and two of my daughters are gone," he'd said. "I don't want you to go too, Marion."

The following week, Leo had given Bud a good job with his company. And now he had bought the two young people a beautiful house in New York City. They were going to live there when they were married. Everything was going to be OK!

On the afternoon of Christmas Eve, Leo Kingship was working in his room at the Kingship Copper offices.

The phone on Leo's desk rang and he answered it.

"There's someone here who wants to talk to you urgently, sir," his secretary said. "His name is Robert Dettweiler."

A moment later, a young man entered the room. He was carrying two books and a newspaper. Leo Kingship looked at him for a moment.

"I've met you before," he said. "But your name isn't Dettweiler."

"You're right, sir," the young man replied. "I'm Gordon Gant. We met at Blue River in March. I thought that you would refuse to see me today, if I told your secretary my real name. I came because I read a story in the newspaper this morning—a story about your daughter's wedding. There's something that I must tell you, sir."

"Mr Gant," Leo said, "please think carefully before you speak. In March, you told me and my daughter Marion about your meeting with Ellen. You told us that my daughter Dorothy had been murdered. You told us Ellen's idea about the old, new, borrowed and blue things which Dorothy had been wearing. But the police said that Dorothy killed herself. And *you* couldn't prove that somebody else had killed her.

"I believe that your reasons for telling us about Ellen's ideas were good reasons—honest reasons," Leo went on. "But the things that you told Marion and me upset us very much. Please don't tell us the same things again now. The police will never find Ellen's killer, and Dorothy killed herself. Marion is going to be married in a few days' time. I want her to be happy, Mr Gant."

"Please listen to me for a minute, sir," Gant said. "I read that your daughter was going to marry Burton Corliss. I remembered that Corliss had been Ellen's boyfriend at Caldwell College. And I wondered if this young man was more interested in your money than in your daughters. Didn't you have that thought too? But then I began to wonder if Corliss had also known Dorothy. I wondered if he had been the father of her child. I didn't know Corliss, but I began to wonder if he had been a student at Stoddard."

"No, I'm sure that he wasn't at Stoddard, Mr Gant," Leo said. "You're a student at Stoddard yourself. You were a second-year student at the same time as Dorothy—you told me that in March. If Corliss had been at Stoddard too, you would have known him."

"That's not true, sir," Gant replied. "Stoddard is a very big university. There are more than twelve thousand students there. Nobody can know all the other students. Ellen thought that I knew Dorothy because we were in the same English class. She was wrong. It was a very big class, and I never spoke to Dorothy. But I told you something important in March. On the evening Ellen died, she left a message for me. The message said that Dorothy's last boyfriend *wasn't* in the English class.

"And this morning," Gant went on, "I remembered something that I read in Ellen's letter to Corliss. She said that she had first met him in the fall of 1950, at Caldwell. But Caldwell is a very small college, sir. There are only about eight hundred students at Caldwell. All the students there know each other. Corliss and Ellen were both third-year students there, but they only met at the beginning of their third year. So Corliss must have come to Caldwell from another college that fall. That's why Ellen didn't meet him earlier.

"This is what I think happened," Gant went on. "Burton Corliss was at Stoddard. He became Dorothy's boyfriend because she was your daughter—he wanted to marry a rich girl. When she became pregnant, he thought that you would be angry. He thought that you would stop giving Dorothy money. So he killed her! Then he moved to Caldwell because he still wanted your money, and he became Ellen's boyfriend. When Ellen discovered that Dorothy had been murdered, Corliss killed her too, and he killed a young man who was helping her. And now Corliss has come to New York. Now he'll get your money, by marrying Marion!"

"You can't prove any of this," Leo said angrily. "Why are

you telling me about it now?"

"I only met Ellen for a few minutes, sir," Gant replied gently. "But I liked her very much. I believe that people should know the truth about her death. And I think that Ellen's killer should be punished.

"And I *can* prove that Corliss was a student at Stoddard," he went on. "When I remembered the words in Ellen's letter, I started to investigate." He opened one of the books that he was carrying. "This is the Stoddard University Yearbook[44] for 1949 to 1950. And here is a picture of Mr Corliss and a list of his classes." He pointed at the page. "He wasn't in Dorothy's English class, but he *was* in her Philosophy and Economics classes! And they were very small classes. He *must* have known her!" Gant opened the other book. "Corliss is in the 1948–9 Yearbook too."

"Oh, God!" Leo said miserably. "Why didn't Marion tell me about this?"

"Perhaps she doesn't know about it," Gant replied. "The newspaper story says that Corliss was at Caldwell, but it says nothing about Stoddard. Why not? Perhaps Corliss hasn't told anybody in New York that he was ever a student there. So perhaps Marion doesn't *know* that he was a student there. And I think that you should tell her. I can't prove that he *killed* Dorothy or Ellen yet. But I can prove that he *knew* Dorothy before he knew Ellen. And you can tell Marion that Mr Corliss is only interested in the Kingship money."

"She won't believe me, Mr Gant," Leo replied. "She doesn't trust me. And she'll say, 'Bud didn't tell me that he knew Dorothy because he didn't want to upset me.' There's nothing more I can do, Mr Gant. Corliss's mother is coming to New York tonight. Marion will marry Corliss on Saturday.

I can't stop it."

"Then I'll have to continue my investigation," Gant said. "Goodbye, Mr Kingship. Thank you for listening to me." He turned and left the room.

———

That evening, Bud's mother arrived in New York. She had dinner at Leo's house. Marion was very happy to meet her. She liked Mrs Corliss very much.

"She's a sweet lady," Marion said to Bud, after his mother had gone back to her hotel. "And you're a wonderful son to her."

Mrs Corliss was going to spend Christmas Day with her son and the Kingships. Then she was going to stay in the city until the wedding, four days later. But she was going to spend the day before the wedding on her own, looking at the buildings of New York City, which she had never visited before. Leo had arranged for Bud, Marion and himself to visit Kingship Copper's smelting works in Illinois on that day. Bud wanted to see the smelting works very much.

———

On the evening of December 27th, Gordon Gant knocked at the door of Leo Kingship's house.

"Why are you here?" Leo said nervously, when he opened the door. "Marion mustn't see you here. If she thinks that I've asked someone to investigate Corliss, she'll never speak to me again."

"Where *is* your daughter, sir?" asked Gant.

"She's gone out with Corliss and his mother," Leo replied. "You can come in for a few minutes, if you have something to tell me."

"Listen to me, sir," Gant said when they were sitting in

Leo's library. "Two days ago, I went to Menasset. I've never broken into[45] anyone's house before. But you told me that Mrs Corliss would be here in New York for Christmas. So I found out her address in Menasset, and I broke into the house. In a closet in Bud Corliss's bedroom, I found a strongbox. I broke it open, sir. And in the box, I found these."

Gant gave Leo some Kingship Copper brochures. They were worn and dirty. They had been read many times!

"And I also found this," Gant went on. He gave Leo the piece of paper on which Bud had written the list of Marion's tastes.

"I don't *know* that you found these in Menasset," said Leo. "You could have got the brochures from my offices. You could have written the list yourself!"

"Phone your offices tomorrow," Gant replied. "Find out if brochures have ever been sent to Mr Burton Corliss. If the answer is yes, find out *when* they were sent."

Leo picked up the phone and dialed a number. "I'll do it now," he said. "There's always somebody working in the New York offices."

A moment later he was talking to his secretary. Then there was silence for three or four minutes. Finally, Leo said, "I understand. Thank you." And he put the phone down.

"You were right, Mr Gant," he said. "I'm sorry that I didn't believe you. Company brochures were sent to Burton Corliss, in Blue River, in early February last year. That was about ten weeks before Dorothy died. He must have made her pregnant soon after he received the brochures." Leo put his hands over his face. "I'll have to tell Marion about this. It won't be easy."

Then suddenly Leo was very angry. "You were right about

"In a closet in Bud Corliss's bedroom, I found a strong-box."

Corliss wanting my money, Mr Gant," he said. "And I think that you were right about Corliss being a murderer too! We can't prove it—the police will never believe us. But if he killed my daughters, he must be punished for it! We have to make him confess[46] to the murders. Will you help me?"

"Yes, I'll help you, sir," said Gant.

"I'll tell Marion about this tonight," said Leo. "*She* must help us too. She mustn't tell Corliss what we know about him. If he finds out about that, he'll escape. He'll disappear. So Marion must pretend that she's going to marry him on Saturday. And tomorrow, we'll go to the smelting works. You must come too, Mr Gant. We'll make Corliss confess there. He won't be able to escape from the smelting works!"

3

The Smelting Works

Bud Corliss was looking out of one of the windows of Kingship Copper's small aircraft. He was feeling wonderful. The sun was shining in the clear blue sky. And now the little plane was descending towards the ground. Far ahead, Bud could see the great Kingship smelting works. Huge clouds of smoke were rising from the roofs of the tall buildings. Dark railroad tracks ran across the shining white snow towards the works. It was all so beautiful. Bud felt that this was the best day of his life!

Leo and Marion were in the plane with him, and there was a young man called Dettweiler too. Leo had told Bud that Dettweiler's father was one of the directors of the company.

Soon, the plane landed in a field near the smelting works. Leo, Marion, Dettweiler and Bud were met by the manager of the works. They all had lunch together in the manager's office, then the manager took Bud and Marion into a room where there were some large photographs. The photographs showed the different processes which were used to make pure copper. The manager talked about this for over an hour. Bud was very interested. He had never been so interested in anything in all his life.

"Leo isn't a young man," he said to himself. "He won't live for many more years. And tomorrow, I'll be his daughter's husband. When Leo dies, all this will be mine!"

At that moment, Leo and Dettweiler came into the room.

"Come up onto one of the catwalks[47] now, Bud," Leo said. "From the catwalks, you can see all the processes below you.

You'll understand everything better then. Marion will stay here."

Leo led Bud and Dettweiler into one of the huge buildings where the smelting processes happened. It was very hot inside the building, and there was smoke everywhere. Leo pointed up towards the roof. The catwalk was a long platform which ran almost the whole length of the building, fifty feet above their heads. It had a metal floor and metal rails along its sides. Leo began to climb a ladder which led to the catwalk. Bud and Dettweiler followed him.

When they reached the catwalk, Leo told Bud to walk in front of Dettweiler and himself. As the three men walked along the metal floor, holding the rails, Leo explained the smelting processes again. As he spoke, he pointed to huge vats of hot, liquid metal on the floor far below them. He explained what was in each vat. He explained how the copper was separated from the other metals which were found with it. Bud asked lots of questions and Leo answered them.

"The catwalk ends over the last vat," Leo said. "The copper in that vat is pure."

A moment later, they reached the end of the catwalk. Bud looked down. Far below him, he saw the huge vat of pure liquid copper. Terrible heat and green smoke were rising from the liquid metal. There was no rail at the end of the catwalk—only an iron chain.

"Do you have any more questions, Bud?" Leo asked.

Bud turned towards the two other men.

"No," he replied. Suddenly he wondered why Leo and Dettweiler were looking so cold and angry.

"Then I have a question for you," said Leo. "How did you make Dorothy write that suicide note?"

"How did you make Dorothy write that suicide note?"

For a moment, Bud couldn't speak. They knew! But *what* did they know? And *how* did they know it?

"I don't understand you, Leo," he said. "I never knew Dorothy. I never met her. I knew Ellen—you know that. But Dorothy was dead when I met Ellen."

"We don't believe you, Corliss," Gant said. "We know that you were a student at Stoddard. We know that you were in two of Dorothy's classes. And we know that you killed her!"

"Who are you, Dettweiler?" Bud said. "Why are you here?"

"I'm here because I knew Ellen," Gant replied. "And my name's not Dettweiler, it's Gant—Gordon Gant. I met Ellen the day before you killed her. I liked her very much."

"Leo, please help me," said Bud. "What is this man talking about? First he said that I knew Dorothy. Then he said that I killed Ellen. Is he crazy?"

"Listen to him, Bud," Leo replied.

"I went to Menasset two days ago," said Gant. "I found your strongbox. I opened it and I found the brochures. And I found the list too, Corliss!"

Bud thought quickly. He turned towards Leo Kingship.

"OK, Leo. OK, OK," he said. "I *did* know Dorothy. I knew her, but I didn't kill her! I've never killed anybody. I confess that I wanted your money. That's why I sent for the brochures. That's why I moved to Caldwell. That's why I moved to New York. Marion won't marry me—I realize that. So I want to leave this place now! I'm going to take my mother back to Menasset tomorrow."

"Turn round, Corliss," Leo said. "Put your hand on the chain."

"Are you crazy too, Leo?" Bud said angrily. But he turned

round and put his hand on the iron chain at the end of the catwalk. As he touched it, the chain broke into two pieces. Now there was nothing to stop anyone falling!

"No, I'm not crazy," Leo said. His voice was cold and hard. "And *you* aren't the only person who can plan a murder, Corliss! We cut the chain while you were talking to the manager. I don't *want* to kill you. I want to take you to the police. I want you to tell *them* what you did. But if you don't confess now that you killed Dorothy and Ellen, we'll push you into the vat of liquid copper. It's very, very hot. You won't live for long, but your last moment will be very painful! Now tell us how you made Dorothy write that note!"

Suddenly, Bud was very afraid. These people really wanted to kill him! He had killed people himself, when he was in the army. And he had killed three people in Blue River. It had been easy to kill them because he hadn't cared about them. But everybody had always cared about *him*. Why didn't *these* people care about him?

Leo stepped towards him. And at the same moment, Bud saw Marion climbing onto the catwalk too. She started to walk towards her father.

"If I confess," Bud thought, "they'll take me to the police. But perhaps I can escape when we're out of this building. If I don't confess, they'll kill me now."

"OK, I did kill Dorothy," he said. "The note was a translation from a Spanish book. I asked her to write it. I killed her and I killed Ellen too!"

He was very afraid, and suddenly he could think only of his fear.

"It was Ellen's fault!" he shouted. "I *told* her not to go to Blue River. I *had* to kill her! And I didn't *want* Dorothy to get pregnant! Everything was *their* fault! Women are so stupid!"

At that moment, Marion pushed past her father and moved towards Bud. The frightened young man turned away from her, and his foot slipped on the metal floor. He started to fall from the end of the catwalk. As he fell towards the terrible vat of liquid copper, he heard a scream. It reminded him of Dorothy's scream as she fell into the air shaft. It reminded him of Ellen's scream before his third bullet killed her. And he realized that the scream was coming from his own mouth.

———

The plane was returning to New York. Marion was crying quietly.

"We weren't really going to kill him, Marion," Gordon Gant said. "We only wanted to make him confess."

"I know that," she said. "I'm not crying for him. But I thought that I was going to be happy at last. You don't understand. You *can't* understand!"

She put her hands over her face.

———

When the Kingships got back to Leo's house, they found Mrs Corliss waiting for them. She looked happy and excited. She smiled at Marion.

"Good evening, my dear," she said. "I'm happy to see you again. Where's Bud?"

Points for Understanding

PART ONE: DOROTHY

1

The young man says that if Leo Kingship finds out about Dorothy's pregnancy, he will stop giving her money. What does the young man know about Dorothy's father which makes him think this?

2

"Now he wanted one of the real Pharmacy students to open the storeroom door for him ... Whoever came would think that the young man was a final-year student—but a student in a different class." Explain why someone would think this.

3

The young man asks Dorothy to translate a passage from a Spanish novel for him. (a) Why? (b) When he writes his note to Dorothy, why does he draw a picture on the other side of it?

4

The young man sees that the sides of the Municipal Building are not completely straight. Why does this worry him?

PART TWO: ELLEN

1

"I've discovered something terrible!" Ellen writes. "Dorothy didn't kill herself—she was murdered." Give a list of Ellen's reasons for thinking this.

2

After she has talked to the Professor of English at Stoddard University, Dorothy writes two names in her notebook. Why does she write these two names?

3

Before she meets Dwight Powell, Ellen thinks that he is probably Dorothy's killer. What does she think about him after her first meeting with him? Why does she think this?

4

Neither of the young men whose names Ellen got from the professor is Dorothy's killer. Ellen has investigated the wrong people. This is because she has made a mistake in her investigation. What was the mistake?

PART THREE: MARION

1

"My favorite artist is ... Charles Demuth," says Bud. Do you think that this is true? Give your reasons.

2

1) Gordon Gant has decided to find out whether Bud Corliss was ever a student at Stoddard University. What has made him take this decision?

2) Marion believes that she and Bud will be happy together. "We like the same books and plays and paintings," she says to her father. "We even like the same food!" She has been pleased and surprised to discover these things. Are *you* surprised? Why/why not?

3

"You *can't* understand!" Marion says to Gordon Gant at the end of the book. What do you think that she means by this?

Glossary

AMERICAN ENGLISH	BRITISH ENGLISH
apartment	flat
attorney	lawyer
checkbook	chequebook
clerk	assistant
closet	cupboard
coffee shop	café
drugstore	chemist's shop
elevator	lift
fall	autumn
guy	man
license	licence
mail/mailbox	letters/post box
purse	handbag
store	shop
story	storey/floor

1 **Municipal Building** (page 5)
   municipal buildings are where the officials for a town or city have
   their offices. For example, the officials for law, health, transport,
   public records, etc. The *Blue River Municipal Library* (page 55) is
   the building where people can read books, or borrow them to
   read in their homes.

2 **permission to marry** (*someone*) (page 6)
   when a young man and a young woman want to get married, the
   man asks the woman's father for *permission to marry* his daughter.
   This is a polite custom.

3 **trailer** (page 6)
   a home that has wheels. *Trailers* are less expensive than houses.
   A trailer can be joined to a car or a truck and moved from one
   place to another. But often trailers stay in a place called a *trailer
   park* (page 14). There are electricity and water systems at trailer
   parks. Sometimes people make gardens around their trailers.

4 *miserably* (page 6)

the young woman is very worried and upset. She is behaving and talking with sadness and fear.

5 *have an abortion*—*to have an abortion* (page 6)

remove an unborn child—a fetus—from a woman's body when it is only a few weeks old. This can be done by giving the woman drugs to end—*abort* (page 11)—the fetus's life. Or the woman can have an *operation* (page 8), when a doctor removes the fetus.

6 *rent*—*to rent* (page 8)

pay someone to live in an apartment or a house. When you are *renting* (page 14), you agree to pay the owner of the property every week, or every month.

7 *take some pills* (page 8)

put the pills in your mouth and swallow them.

8 *drugstore* (page 8)

a place where medicines and many others things can be bought. Food can be bought and eaten in American drugstores. They were often popular places for young people to meet.

9 *Pharmacy Laboratory* (page 8)

the building where university students learn to make medicines.

10 *make love with* (*someone*) (page 8)

have sex with someone.

11 *Economics and Philosophy* (page 9)

economics is the study of how governments, businesses and people make decisions about money. *Philosophy* is the study of knowledge and thinking.

12 *brochures* (page 9)

documents which give information about a company and how much money it has earned. *Brochures* give a company's address and describe its offices. There are often illustrations—drawings, photographs and charts—to show what products the company sells and how these are made.

13 *smelting works* (page 9)

the factory that is owned by Leo Kingship. In these large buildings, pieces of rock which contain metal are broken. The crushed rock is then put into extremely hot ovens. The rock burns and melts and the metals which are inside it come out. The *hot liquid metals* (page 82) are then heated again, cooled and poured into containers called *vats* (page 82). These *processes* (page 81) are repeated until everything is removed except the *pure copper* (page 81). In this way, the copper has been *separated* (page 82) from the other metals in the rock.

14 *possessive* (page 10)

a *possessive* person does not allow someone that he/she loves to be with other people. This kind of behaviour is called *possessiveness* (page 10).

15 *broken up with*—*to break up with (someone)*(page 10)

finish a friendship or a relationship. You no longer spend time with that person.

16 *divorce*—*to divorce (someone)* (page 10)

Mr and Mrs Kingship did not have a happy marriage. Mr Kingship decided to end the marriage and get a *divorce*. Husbands and wives are *divorced* after they go to a court and a judge decides to end the marriage.

17 *work*—*if the pills work* (page 11)

the young man hopes that taking the pills will be successful and that they will abort the fetus. A plan that *is going to work* is going to be successful (page 5).

18 *throw up*—*to throw up* (page 12)

be sick, vomit.

19 *toxicology* (page 15)

toxicology is the study of poisons. Poisons are things that can make you ill, or kill you if you eat or drink them. Poisons can be found in some minerals, animals and plants. The *lethal dose* (page 19) of a poison is the amount that can kill a person.

20 *bulletin board* (page 16)

the place on a wall where notices and messages are attached for people to read.

21 *bunch of keys* (page 17)

a *bunch of* means some, several, a number of. A *bunch of keys* is a number of keys held together on a metal ring.

22 *gelatin capsules* (page 17)

soft pills which can be pulled open and filled with medicine. When you swallow the capsules, the soft gelatin breaks open inside your stomach.

23 *suicide note* (page 19)

the message that somebody writes before they kill themselves. A *suicide note* sometimes gives the reasons why that person is so unhappy.

24 *solution* *(to a problem)* (page 19)

the way to end a problem or a difficulty.

25 *suspicious—to be suspicious* (page 19)
think that there is something wrong, or believe that someone is
behaving in a strange way.

26 *typewriters* (page 22)
machines that were used to print documents before computers
were used. A person puts a piece of paper into a *typewriter*, presses
the letters and the numbers on the keyboard and *types* (page 22) a
document onto the paper.

27 *telephone booth* (page 25)
a tall box that people go into to make telephone calls. Telephone
booths are found on streets, in stores, hotels and restaurants and
in railroad stations and airports. At the time of this story, you
picked up the phone and spoke to an *operator* (page 28). The
operator worked for the phone company. For some calls, the
operator connected you to the person you wished to speak to.

28 *mailbox* (page 25)
a box that letters are put into. They are *mailed* or delivered to the
address on the envelope.

29 *University Office* (page 26)
the building on a campus where records of the students are kept.

30 *Marriage License Bureau* (page 27)
before people can get married, they need a document called *a
marriage license*. This paper gives information about the man and
the woman. They go to an official, who asks them questions
before they get married. *The Marriage License Bureau* is the office
where people go to get a license.

31 *birth certificate* (page 28)
a document which gives your name, the date of your birth, and
the address where you were born. Your *birth certificate* also gives
the names of your parents.

32 *lobby* (page 29)
the area inside the entrance of an office building or an apartment
building.

33 *air shaft* (page 30)
the tall building has offices on each of its four sides, but there is
an *air shaft*—a tall space—in the center. The windows in the
middle of the building can be opened so that air from the shaft
can move into all the rooms.

34 *checkbooks* (page 41)

books which your bank gives you when you put money into a bank account. If you want to take money out of your account to pay for something, you write your instructions onto a check. Then you tear the check out of the checkbook and give it to the person you wish to pay. Checkbooks show how much money you have taken out of the bank account and who you have paid.

35 *personal files* (page 42)

folders with information about each student studying at the university, including date of birth, names, family addresses and test scores. The files also list which courses the students are studying. The files might also include the students' interests and medical records.

36 *disc jockey* (page 44)

a person who works at a radio station and plays music on radio shows. There were no cassettes or CDs at this time. Music was played from plastic discs called records.

37 *swear on this Bible*—*to swear on a Bible* (page 51)

the Bible is the holy book of Christians. *To swear on a Bible* means that you hold the book, and make a promise to tell the truth.

38 *coffee shop* (page 51)

a place where people can meet and drink coffee together.

39 *attorney* (page 55)

a lawyer. A person who knows all the rules of the law.

40 *screens* (page 58)

tall, flat pieces of furniture that can be carried from place to place so that people can have private meetings. The screens can be put between tables so that people at one table cannot see the people at the table beside them.

41 *tastes* (page 62)

the types of things that Marion likes. The clothes that you like to wear, the decoration of your house, the music that you listen to, the food that you enjoy—these are all examples of your *tastes*.

42 *advertising agency* (page 62)

a company that helps you to sell your products. Advertisements tell people about your company or your products. Advertising agencies prepare advertisements that go into newspapers and magazines and onto radio and TV.

43 *director* (*of an agency*) (page 62)

an important person in a company or business.

44 Stoddard University Yearbook (page 76)
American colleges prepare a book each year which gives the names and photographs of the students who are studying there. It also says which classes they are in.

45 broken into—*to break into (something/somewhere)* (page 78)
break a door or a window of a house and go inside. If the house is not yours, this is a crime.

46 confess—*to make someone confess to (something)* (page 80)
Leo Kingship wants to make Bud tell the truth and say that he murdered Dorothy, Ellen and Dwight.

47 catwalks (page 81)
flat narrow paths of metal with metal rails along each side. *Catwalks* are usually found high inside a building, near the roof. People can walk along these paths and look down at the work being done in the factory, far below them. See the illustration on page 83.

Published by Macmillan Heinemann ELT
Between Towns Road, Oxford OX4 3PP
Macmillan Heinemann ELT is an imprint of
Macmillan Publishers Limited
Companies and representatives throughout the world

ISBN 0 333 798856

This retold version by F.H. Cornish for Macmillan Guided Readers
First published 2000
Text © Macmillan Publishers Limited 2000,2002
Design and illustration © Macmillan Publishers Limited 2000, 2002
Heinemann is a registered trademark of Reed Educational and Professional Publishing Ltd.
This version first published 2002

Illustrated by Shirley Belwood
Map on page 3 and illustrations on page 6 and 7 by John Gilkes
Cover Martin Macrae and Marketplace Design

Printed in China

2006 2005 2004 2003 2002
11 10 9 8 7 6 5 4 3 2